THE ESSENTIAL BONSAI

THE ESSENTIAL BONSAI

Ken Norman

Photography by John Freeman

HERMES
HOUSE

This edition published by Hermes House,
an imprint of Anness Publishing Limited
Hermes House, 88–89 Blackfriars Road, London SE1 8HA

© Anness Publishing Limited 1998
Updated © 2002

Published in the USA by Hermes House, Anness Publishing Inc.
27 West 20th Street, New York, NY 10011

Publisher: Joanna Lorenz
Project Editor: Fiona Eaton
Designer: Lilian Lindblom
Photography: John Freeman
Illustrations: Anna Koska
Additional pictures: Ken Norman pp11, 16, 17, 18, 19

1 3 5 7 9 10 8 6 4 2

This book is an extract edition of Ken Norman's larger work
Step-by-Step Create Your Own Bonsai

Contents

Introduction

It is not necessary to have expert knowledge to get started in the art and culture of bonsai. If you are already growing plants or trees in containers you will have mastered some of the basic techniques, such as branch pruning, root pruning, shaping and feeding. Bonsai is all about making miniature versions of mature trees. The tree is just one component of the composition – the other is the pot or container, which must be complementary in size, shape and colour, just as a frame complements a painting.

The first step is to choose a tree or plant that has the potential of becoming a good bonsai, growing and training it so that it blends with the container to give an authentic impression of nature in miniature. The beauty of bonsai lies in the balance and harmony between the tree and the pot. Although a bonsai can be as little as 2.5 cm (1 in) or as much as 125 cm (4 ft) tall, it will always create the illusion of a mature, full-size tree.

Buying a so-called ready-made bonsai could be just the beginning of a pastime that may well become an obsession. This book is intended to teach you the basic skills required to grow and train your own bonsai, and to achieve the pleasure of knowing that it has been all your own work.

Apex must give the impression of being sculpted by the natural elements.

Upper branch structure must blend with the lower branches.

Space between branches is important aesthetically. It also allows light into the branch structure.

Jin – dead branch.

The lowest branch should normally be the heaviest.

A strong, surface root structure and trunk buttress will give the tree a mature image.

The soil surface must look natural and can be enhanced by the addition of moss, lichen or very small plants.

The pot must harmonize with the tree. This tree has a rugged, primitive appearance and so the pot must exhibit similar characteristics.

The depth of the pot should be approximately the same as the diameter of the trunk.

The History of Bonsai

The first bonsai trees from China and Japan were almost certainly trees collected from the wild mountainous regions of these two countries, which were planted in ceramic pots and displayed somewhere around the outside of people's homes. These were trees that had been dwarfed naturally by the harsh conditions of their high mountain habitats. The earliest mention of bonsai in Japan appears in records of the Kasuga Shrine in the Kamakura period (1192–1333), and there are picture scrolls showing bonsai from the same period. These scrolls actually depicted daily scenes during the Heian period (794–1191), therefore suggesting that the culture of bonsai existed in Japan as early as 1,200 years ago. It was not until the beginning of the 20th century that bonsai were seen outside Japan, when they appeared at an exhibition in London in 1909 and caused a sensation. In the last 40 years bonsai has grown in popularity throughout the world. Local, national and international bonsai clubs collaborate to advance bonsai knowledge worldwide.

8

The origins of bonsai are somewhat shrouded in the mists of time, but the first bonsai are thought to have been grown in China about 1,500 years ago. About 1,200 years ago, these miniature trees began to gain popularity in Japan.

Right: A 95-year-old Japanese white pine (Pinus pentaphylla)*, which has grown to a height of 97 cm (38 in).*

Buying a Bonsai

When buying a bonsai tree from a specialist shop, make sure that the tree you select looks healthy and that the rest of the trees in the shop or nursery look equally good. Check that the tree is firm in the pot. If it isn't, it will only recently have been repotted and should be left alone. Check the soil to see that it is a good open mix and not waterlogged. The tree may have wire on the trunk and branches, but as long as it is not cutting into the bark it should be all right.

If you buy from a bonsai centre, ask as many questions about the trees as possible. Bonsai experts are always glad to share their knowledge, and their advice and tips are invaluable if you are purchasing your first bonsai. Bonsai can be an expensive hobby because it may take many years to produce a good quality tree, but you need not spend too much to acquire your first tree. It is best to start with an inexpensive tree so that you can learn as you go along.

A bonsai collection can be started from seeds or cuttings, but this can be a slow process. To achieve quicker results, buy suitable material from nurseries or garden centres.

So-called "finished bonsai" can be purchased from garden centres, nurseries and supermarkets, but for better quality trees and expert advice it is best to go to a good bonsai nursery or shop.

9

Right: Four trees displayed in a small space on two different types of timber stands.

Choosing and Displaying Bonsai

Whatever your climate, it is generally trees that grow naturally outdoors in your area that are suitable as outdoor bonsai, whereas those that come from different regions need to be kept in a controlled environment. In temperate areas, indoor trees normally need to be kept in warmer conditions with fairly high humidity. This can often be difficult to achieve in centrally-heated homes. They also need good light conditions, but should not be subjected to direct sunlight through a window, as this could result in burnt foliage. The techniques used for training, styling and general maintenance of both indoor and outdoor bonsai are the same.

10

DISPLAYING BONSAI INDOORS
Take great care when displaying your bonsai inside the home, to see that everything involved in the display complements and enhances the appearance of the tree.

Good-quality display tables are available commercially and can be bought in a variety of shapes and sizes. But if you feel that you have the skill and ability, you may be able to make a stand yourself. Bamboo matting, gravel and many other materials may be used in the display of bonsai. If you need some inspiration there are many books on Japanese design and culture.

Once you have decided either to buy or to grow a tree as a bonsai, you need to be sure that you select a type of tree that suits the environment in which it is going to be kept, in other words, indoors or outdoors.

Above: An antique stand with a cascade-style Juniperus procumbens.

Above: A rosewood stand with Juniperus squamata *"Meyeri".*

OUTDOOR DISPLAY

For bonsai kept outside, timber benches treated with preservative are ideal, and can be supported either on timber legs or concrete blocks. The latter will remove the possibility of rot setting in or the benches collapsing.

Strong benching is important, and you should also see that the size and weight of benching is kept in proportion to the trees displayed. The best height for displaying bonsai is roughly eye level so that the trees can be seen at their best. This may not always be possible if you have a large collection, and it would be a good idea to vary the height of each stand to suit each tree. The main aim should be to give a pleasing overall effect while providing you with ease of access for maintenance.

Above: The author's bonsai display in Sussex, England.

Pots and Containers

Pots for bonsai trees must be frost-proof if they are to be used outdoors, and therefore must be made from stoneware. Pots made of other materials such as plastic and mica will be fine, but are best suited for use by beginners and as training pots. Most people will graduate to stoneware pots eventually, because they give the trees a far superior appearance.

Make sure that the pots you choose have adequate drainage holes – usually quite large – so that excess water can drain away easily. Some pots may have a series of small holes around the perimeter of the base which can be used to tie the tree into the pot. Also check that the base of the pot is flat so that there are no areas where water may become trapped. All pots should have feet so that the base of the pot stands clear of the display stand. This allows for free airflow around the base of the pot, and will promote the health of the tree. Bonsai pots should be unglazed on the inside as this helps to keep the tree stable in the pot, especially when the roots have grown sufficiently to come into contact with the sides.

12

The bonsai pot is not just the container in which to grow your bonsai; it is most important that it complements the tree so that the final composition is aesthetically satisfying. Bonsai pots come in many different shapes, sizes and colours to suit all styles.

The blue oval container is ideal for indoor bonsai such as serissa or ficus.

A tall pot such as this one is ideal for cascade bonsai because it allows the form of the cascading tree to be seen at its best.

A round, dark pot such as this one will enhance a literati bonsai.

A shallow oval pot is best suited to deciduous varieties.

A round pot, with its decorative rim, complements a flowering tree such as a malus or even a literati pine.

A rectangular matt brown pot is a suitable container for coniferous bonsai such as pines or junipers.

A square matt pot is ideal for a cascade juniper.

Soil for Bonsai

The function of soil is to retain sufficient water and nutrients to maintain a regular supply of these to the roots of the tree. The soil mixture must be open to ensure free drainage and it must contain air spaces to enable the roots to breathe. The soil must also securely anchor the tree in the pot, and should therefore be substantial and dense enough to do this. A good general-purpose soil mix would be: 1 part humus matter; 1 part loam; 2 parts sharp grit. Make sure you find a suitable grit, as you need one that has sharp angular particles, but not sharp slivers that can cause damage to roots. Instead of loam, you can use a commercial potting compost, but remember this already contains some nutrients.

All soil ingredients should be dry when mixed, and passed through a sieve to give particles of between 2 and 5 mm (⅛ and ¼ in). Some particles finer than this will tend to clog the air spaces and hinder the healthy development of a good root system.

Other soil mixtures, imported from Japan, are perhaps more suited to the experienced grower, but they provide excellent growing conditions for trees and many other plants. Of the three varieties available, Akadama is a general-purpose soil, Kanuma is suitable for ericaceous plants such as azaleas, and Kiryu is ideal for pines and junipers.

Rather than mixing fertilizers with the soil when potting, it is more satisfactory to add them when necessary during the year. Feeding is dealt with in more detail later in this book.

Bonsai can be grown in any type of soil, but they may survive only for short periods if the mix is not suitable. The correct mix of two or three different ingredients is crucial if your bonsai is going to remain healthy for any length of time.

13

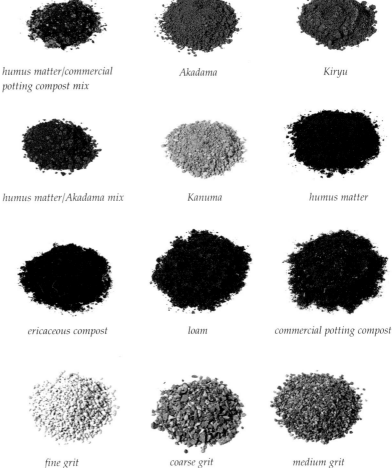

humus matter/commercial potting compost mix

Akadama

Kiryu

humus matter/Akadama mix

Kanuma

humus matter

ericaceous compost

loam

commercial potting compost

fine grit

coarse grit

medium grit

Tools and Equipment

The essential tools for growing and caring for your bonsai are large and small scissors, secateurs (pruners), wire cutters, old chopsticks for working soil around the roots when repotting, and an old fork with its prongs bent to use as a rake. These tools will do most jobs, but as you gain experience you may want to build up a set of specialist Japanese tools, which will make a much better job.

PRUNING

The first tools that most people find useful are a pair of pointed scissors and a pair of heavy-duty scissors for pruning the roots. Branch cutters, which make a concave cut that encourages the wound to heal over more quickly, might be your next purchase, followed by a pair of knob cutters, which are used to remove a branch or a branch stub close to the trunk. Special scissors are also available for trimming shoots and leaves. A strong, short-bladed gardener's knife is ideal for cutting into bark when making *jin*. All these tools should be sharp for making good clean cuts, and free of dirt, to reduce the possibility of introducing disease into wounds.

TRAINING

For positioning trunks and branches, annealed copper is the traditional wire used, but in recent years plain or anodized aluminium has taken preference because it is easy to use and can be recycled without heat treatment. The gauge needs to be thick enough to hold the branch in place after bending.

A large variety of specialist equipment is available for bonsai, but to get started just a few basic tools are all that is required.

POTTING

When repotting bonsai, you will need a sieve for preparing soil, and plastic mesh to cover the drainage holes in the pots. A scoop is useful for adding soil, and pliers are essential when tying trees into pots with wire.

CARE AND MAINTENANCE

A coco brush is useful for tidying the soil surface and cleaning up, while a toothbrush is the perfect tool for cleaning trunks and branches. Tweezers help with fiddly tasks such as the removal of old pine needles. When pruning, apply a special bonsai sealer to all wounds to prevent fungal infection.

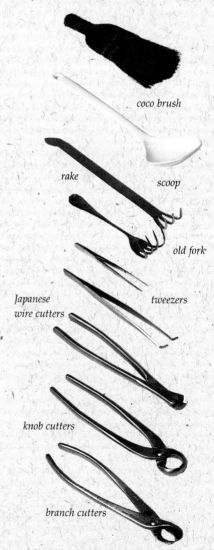

coco brush

rake

scoop

old fork

Japanese wire cutters

tweezers

knob cutters

branch cutters

14

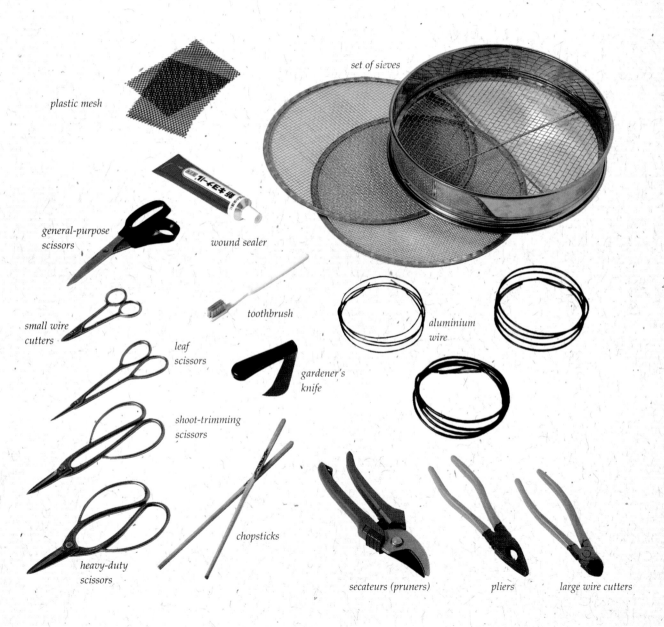

plastic mesh

set of sieves

general-purpose
scissors

wound sealer

small wire
cutters

toothbrush

aluminium
wire

leaf
scissors

gardener's
knife

shoot-trimming
scissors

chopsticks

heavy-duty
scissors

secateurs (pruners)

pliers

large wire cutters

In early spring your trees will begin to grow once more following their dormant period in the winter months. This is the busiest part of the year.

Most of your deciduous trees should have been repotted in late winter, but if you have any still to be done attend to them as soon as possible, before the buds break. If there is any chance of hard frosts, you should protect freshly potted trees by placing them in a shed or cold greenhouse until weather conditions improve.

You can begin to do some pruning now, as this is the best time of the year to tidy up deciduous trees. Without the leaves, it is easy to see which twigs or branches need removing. If shoots begin to extend, trim them back to one or two pairs of leaves to maintain a compact growth pattern.

You will be able to apply wire to conifers, such as pine and juniper, but preferably not deciduous trees; leave these until later in the year. Keep a close watch on the wire on trees at all times of the year and remove it if it looks as if it is cutting into the bark.

Do not apply fertilizer to recently potted trees, because it will tend to burn any roots that were pruned during the repotting process. Watering will probably be necessary in moderate amounts as the weather warms up slightly, but be careful not to overwater freshly potted trees.

Above: An Acer palmatum – *a small leaf variety of Japanese maple – in spring. The tree is approximately 30 years old and has reached a height of 35 cm (14 in).*

Summer

Your trees will be getting well into growth by now and shoots need to be trimmed regularly. Continue to trim deciduous trees back to one or two pairs of leaves and pinch out buds on conifers as they extend.

Repotting should have been completed by late winter, but if you have a tree that appears to be too large for the pot, just lift it out and plant it in a more suitable pot. However, do not disturb the roots: just place it in the pot and fill the gaps with soil.

Wire can be applied to any tree at this time of year, but remember to check on wire applied earlier in the season, and remove it if you think the branch may have set in place.

You will need to water almost every day as the weather becomes warmer. If it is very hot, you may need to water more than once each day. In any case, check the soil regularly. Feeding will be required for most trees throughout the summer, but reduce the amount of nitrogen applied in late summer.

Above left: An Acer palmatum *in early summer, with its distinctive seasonal foliage.*
Above right: The same tree photographed in late summer, when its leaves have faded to green.

Autumn

18

The growth rate of trees slows down to almost nothing in early autumn, and the leaves on deciduous trees begin to fall. Root growth slows down and the buds that have already formed for next year harden up to prepare for the winter.

You can continue to prune pines, but it is best not to prune deciduous trees at this time of year because it may induce a spurt of growth that could be severely damaged by an early frost. As growth has come to a stop, trimming of shoots will not be necessary, except for junipers and Cryptomeria, which may require shoots pinched for the last time.

You will not generally need to wire in the autumn, but you must keep a close watch on conifers as they have a late burst of growth, and may suffer damage from wire that is left in place. It is not advisable to apply wire in late autumn; in fact, it is beneficial to remove it so that the trees can have a bit of a rest during the winter months.

As the weather cools, there will not be the need to water so often, but check the condition of the soil daily and water sparingly if required. Remember that a strong wind can dry the soil just as quickly as strong sun. Apply two doses of nitrogen-free fertilizer, one in early and one in mid-autumn, to harden off the current year's growth. This will help to protect your trees over the winter.

As the leaves fall, remove them from the soil surface and display benches so that you do not leave any hiding places for unwanted insects and other pests.

Above: A group of Zelkova serrata *in autumn foliage.*

Winter

Winter may be a quiet time for your trees, but quite a bit of maintenance work is needed and, unless you live in a mild area, you may need to protect your trees from severe weather conditions.

Pruning and wiring should not be carried out in early winter, but as deciduous trees are now free of leaves, it is a good time to study the tree's form to assess which branches may need pruning or adjusting next year.

Trees kept outdoors should not need watering, because rain, mist and dew will supply enough water. If they become too wet, place them under cover, in the open, to dry out a little. They will not be harmed by being covered with snow: it will keep the root ball at an even temperature. Clear snow from the branches to avoid damage.

Prepare for spring by buying pots and soil. Mix and sift the soil, and make sure all the ingredients are to hand. Start repotting in late winter and protect freshly potted trees from frost.

Above: A group of Zelkova serrata in winter. These trees are approximately 30 years old and 69 cm (27 in) high.

Propagation from Seed

Select species to grow from seed with small leaves or needles and make sure that the seeds you buy are fresh. If your seeds have a hard case, you will have to chip or crack them to encourage germination, and hardy tree seeds will need to be stratified before they germinate. This involves chilling them to simulate frosty conditions. Mix the seeds with slightly damp sand or peat and place them in the salad compartment of a refrigerator for three or four weeks before sowing. Some seeds may take two or three years to germinate, so you will need to be patient. Your soil should consist of finer particles than normal bonsai mixture and have about 50 per cent sand.

You will need
- seed tray
- soil
- seeds
- pressure board
- plant sprayer containing water and fungicide
- Perspex cover

Although growing from seed is the slowest way of producing a bonsai, it can be very rewarding. You will know the exact age of your plants and be able to train some as bonsai from the beginning, while growing others to become larger plants for styling as bonsai.

1 Fill a seed tray with soil and lay the seeds on the surface, spacing them evenly. Cover with a layer of soil that is approximately the same thickness as the seeds.

2 Press the surface down lightly with the pressure board to secure the seeds in place. Spray with water that has had a fungicide added to help prevent rotting.

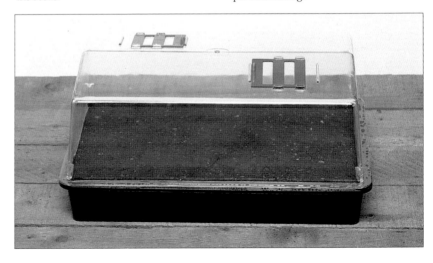

3 Cover the completed tray with the Perspex cover and place it outdoors, if the seeds are from hardy trees, or indoors in a warm place, if they are tropical or indoor varieties.

Propagation from Cuttings

Hardwood and softwood cuttings are the two types normally taken when starting bonsai. Softwood cuttings are taken in early summer and hardwood cuttings are taken in the autumn.

YOU WILL NEED
- cuttings
- scissors
- seed tray
- soil
- chopstick
- plant sprayer containing water and fungicide
- Perspex cover

Propagating from seed may give some variation in leaf shape or colour. If you propagate from cuttings, you will get the same characteristics as the original plant.

1 For broad-leaf trees, take a cutting that has several nodes and cut off the lowest leaves and the growing tip.

2 For conifers, take a heel cutting by pulling down on the shoot until it becomes detached.

2 1

3 Having filled a tray with very sandy soil, make a small hole with a chopstick for each cutting. Insert the cuttings into the soil for about one-third of their length. Push some soil around the cutting. Spray with a mix of water and fungicide.

4 Cover the tray to retain humidity and place outdoors in a shady place.

Pruning Deciduous Trees

Basic pruning can be done using an ordinary pair of scissors. When removing a branch, use a pair of concave cutters, and prune close to the trunk. If a small stub is left after pruning, remove it using a knob cutter. When pruning Japanese maples, never trim back shoots to the next bud. Always leave 1 cm (½ in) of shoot to allow for die-back.

YOU WILL NEED
- scissors
- branch cutters
- knob cutter (optional)
- wound sealer

Pruning must be carried out with care, so that the wound heals leaving little or no scar on the trunk or branch.

1 Remove twigs or branches that are crossing or growing inwards.

2 Tidy up any unsightly knobbly pieces using branch cutters.

3 Apply a special bonsai sealer to all wounds to prevent fungal infection.

22

Left: Acer palmatum

Pruning Conifers

When removing a branch from a conifer, you can leave a substantial length of the branch intact and use it to enhance the tree by creating a *jin*, or natural-looking dead branch. When pruning back conifer branches, always leave some foliage on the end of the branch so that there is something to draw the sap.

YOU WILL NEED
- scissors
- branch cutters
- wound sealer

Most techniques for pruning deciduous trees apply to conifers, but there are one or two exceptions.

1 Cut out any upward-growing secondary branches using scissors.

2 Remove small branches near the trunk and apply wound sealer.

3 Pinch out the tips of shoots using your fingers.

Right: Juniperus chinensis

23

Annual Pruning

For trees in training, you may be able to leave some of these shoots in place, if you need to thicken the adjacent trunk or branch, but in mature trees you should remove them as soon as possible. You will need to cut back unwanted growth during the dormant season to allow the tree to develop in the required shape. Prune out branches that are too thick for the design, trimming back to a dormant bud pointing in the required direction of the growth where possible.

In mature trees, tidying up old pruning cuts, removing dead branches and thinning out the branch structure are all essential to ensure continued improvement of your bonsai. The relationship of one branch to another and the space between them is important, because this enables the tree to be seen at its best. Creating spaces between branches also allows the sunlight to reach all the foliage and this will lead to healthier, more compact growth.

You will need
• scissors

Every year your trees will produce an abundance of shoots from their leaf axils, which if left in place would eventually dominate the appearance of your bonsai.

Above: Larix leptolepis

1 Using scissors prune the shoots on the lower branches, leaving one or two buds.

2 Repeat the process on all the other branches of the tree.

24

Pruning Shoots

Maintain the shape of your bonsai by pinching or cutting out the growing tips during the spring and summer.

Broad-leaf trees generally produce shoots with pairs of leaves or single leaves on alternating sides of the branch. Conifers vary widely in the appearance of their tip growth, but the pruning technique for each is similar. Spruce and some junipers form small bunches of needles that can be removed using your fingers. Each week, remove the largest shoots, but make sure there is always some fresh growth remaining. On maples and some other broad-leaf trees, you can remove all the leaves in late spring when they are fully developed. This encourages the tree to produce a second, smaller set of leaves, but should only be carried out once in two years, and then only if the tree is healthy.

YOU WILL NEED
• scissors

1 With conifers such as this juniper, hold each shoot with two fingers and pinch out the tip.

2 For pruning harder shoots use scissors; angle them so that they follow the angle of the needles.

Left:
Ulmus parvifolia

3 Pinch out the soft tips of deciduous trees in a similar way to that used for conifers. Prune woody shoots using scissors, leaving one or two leaves.

25

Shaping by Wiring

The wiring technique is straightforward, but requires practice to master. Practise on branches of varying thickness from any tree or shrub before you start on a serious project. Check the flexibility of branches before applying any wire, as some species are more brittle than others. Young branches are usually more flexible than older ones. The wire should run neatly on the trunk or branch at an angle of about 45 degrees, and should not be too tight or too loose. Having the correct type of cutters is a great help, as they will enable you to cut the wire close to the tree without damaging the bark. When styling a bonsai, make sure you position every branch and twig. It is this attention to detail in the initial stages that could make the difference between a mediocre and a successful shape.

<u>2 6</u>

YOU WILL NEED
- wire
- small wire cutters
- large wire cutters
- scissors

Wiring is one of the most important techniques of bonsai training, because it enables the trunk, branches and shoots to be positioned precisely.

1 Do a trial run. Wind on a length of wire about half the thickness of the branch. Using your thumbs to support the branch, slowly and gently bend it until the required shape is reached. Stop if the branch begins to crack.

2 When wiring a trunk, anchor the wire by pushing the end into the soil at the base of the trunk. The wire should run at about 45 degrees to the trunk.

3 If there are two branches near each other, one piece of wire can be used to deal with them both. In this way the wire on each branch will help to anchor the other branch in position.

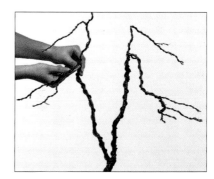

4 Having applied wire to every branch, position them so that a mature appearance is obtained.

Opposite: Betula pendula aureum

Root Preparation and Pruning

The root structure must always be young, healthy and free from disease, and this is achieved by the regular replacement of soil and pruning of the root system. How often these tasks will have to be carried out depends upon the species and age of the tree. Pruning the roots will encourage many more young feeder roots to develop, which will lead to healthy growth in the upper part of the tree. Root pruning and repotting should be carried out in late winter or early spring, just before, or just as, the roots begin to grow, to minimize the chance of the roots rotting. After repotting, the soil should be kept moist so that the tree is able to support new roots without the fear of waterlogging.

28

YOU WILL NEED
• chopstick
• rake
• scissors

The roots of a bonsai are the most important part of the plant. They are responsible for providing the tree with water and nutrients, so it is important that you care for the roots properly.

1 Carefully remove the tree from the pot. This tree has a plentiful root system that needs pruning to encourage new root growth.

2 A chopstick is ideal for untangling the thicker roots.

3 Using a rake, comb the roots to remove about one-third of the soil around the roots.

4 Trim the roots from the sides of the root system using sharp scissors.

5 Cut away excess roots from the underside of the tree, so that the root pad is flat.

6 The final appearance should be neat and have sufficient fibrous roots to support the tree when repotted.

Right: Juniperus rigida

29

Preparing Pots and Potting

The drainage holes in the bottom of a bonsai pot should be covered with plastic mesh to stop the soil falling through. This also prevents certain pests from entering the soil through the holes. A layer of small stones or coarse grit should be spread over the bottom of the pot to allow free drainage. When placing the tree in the pot, it is a good idea to make a mound of soil under the root ball, so that when you settle the tree down you know that the roots will be in good contact with the soil. Twist the tree around, clockwise and anticlockwise, when you are potting, because this also helps to ensure a good contact between roots and soil. When adding new soil, work it in carefully around all the roots with a chopstick.

30

YOU WILL NEED
• wire
• mesh
• pot
• scoop
• coarse grit or Akadama
• soil
• chopstick

Pots should always be clean and dry. If you are reusing pots, clean them with a stiff brush and clean water, and rinse and dry them before use.

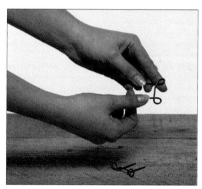

1 Prepare a short length of wire into a "butterfly" shape for each drainage hole by twisting it.

2 Place a piece of mesh over each drainage hole. Push the free ends of the "butterfly" through the mesh and drainage hole, and bend them back beneath the pot.

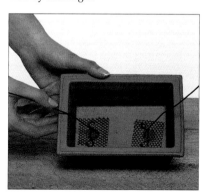

3 Large pots may have small holes in the base, which can be used to secure the tree in the pot with wire. If the pot does not have these, pass the wire through the drainage holes.

4 Using a scoop, cover the bottom of the pot with coarse grit or coarse Akadama to provide a drainage layer.

5 Add a small amount of soil and settle the tree on to the soil firmly.

6 Bring the two ends of the tie-in wires together and twist to secure the tree. Top up with soil and tidy the surface of the soil.

Right: Juniperus rigida

31

Watering

The frequency of watering will depend on many things. A strong wind or sun, or a combination of both, can quickly dry out the soil, so you must monitor moisture levels in the soil regularly. Indoor trees require slightly different watering techniques. It is easy to water by just "dunking" the whole pot into a bowl, completely covering the soil with water. Wait until the bubbles stop rising, remove from the water and allow to drain. Indoor trees can also be watered using a small watering-can. Indoor trees often also require extra humidity around the foliage. To achieve this, spray the leaves regularly or place the pot on a shallow dish or tray containing a layer of absorbent granules, which are kept wet, so that as the water evaporates it drifts up and around the foliage.

YOU WILL NEED
• bowl
• watering-can
• sprayer

If your trees are kept outside where rain can water them, you need to worry only when it does not rain. Use a watering-can with a fine rose or if you have a large collection of trees use a hose, which should also have a fine rose attached.

1 To water an indoor bonsai, fill a bowl with water and immerse the pot in the water until the bubbles cease to rise. Remove from the water and leave to drain.

2 Alternatively, use a watering-can with a fine rose attached to water the soil and roots.

3 The same watering-can may be used to water the foliage on a weekly basis, particularly if there has not been any rain for a while.

4 You can also water with a pressure sprayer or with a hose fitted with a fine rose to create humidity around the leaves.

Feeding

Fertilizers come in a variety of forms. Pellets are a slow-release fertilizer and will take care of feeding requirements for several weeks at a time. Soluble powder and liquid feeds are applied to the soil with a watering-can. Foliar feed can be applied with a sprayer.

Feed from early spring to late summer. In autumn feed with a low – or no – nitrogen content to help the tree through the winter.

Most fertilizers contain nitrogen (N), phosphorus (P) and potassium (K). Nitrogen is essential for leaf and stem growth. Too much nitrogen will make the tree produce too much long growth. Use a balanced fertilizer with a fairly low nitrogen content. Phosphorus promotes healthy root growth, helps the growth of buds, and protects against disease and adverse winter conditions. Potassium (potash) encourages the formation of flowers and fruit, and is vital in the fight against disease.

Most commercial fertilizers contain all three main nutrients plus some trace elements. There is one type of fertilizer that is normally only obtainable from bonsai nurseries, which has an NPK ratio of 0:10:10. This is an autumn feed, which will harden off the current season's growth in readiness for the winter.

YOU WILL NEED
- fertilizer – liquid, granules, pellets
- watering-can

Regular feeding at the correct time of year, with the correct fertilizer, is essential to maintain good healthy growth. A certain amount of fertilizer is washed out by watering, so a regular input of nutrients is required.

BONSAI TIP
Never apply more fertilizer than the recommended dose.

1 You can apply liquid fertilizers to the roots using a watering-can. Tip the fertilizer into the can.

33

2 Make sure the fertilizer has been absorbed into the water, then apply the mixture to the soil.

3 Pellets made of rapeseed cake can be applied by laying them on the soil surface, then watering.

Insect Pests

Most pests can be kept under control by hygienic practices, which will avoid the excessive use of insecticides.

Scale insect

Scale insects can be inconspicuous until they begin to produce eggs. When this happens, the limpet-like shells lift and a white, fluffy, sticky mass appears from beneath. Combat them with systemic insecticide and pick off the large adult insects. A cotton bud (swab) soaked in methylated spirit (denatured alcohol) can be very effective for rubbing scale from the trunks of bonsai.

Scale insect (Hemiptera: Coccoidea)

Aphids

Aphids come in many forms, but greenfly, blackfly and whitefly are the most common. They can be treated with a systemic insecticide. The most troublesome pest for indoor bonsai may be whitefly, but regular applications of insecticide will control the pest.

Greenfly, blackfly and whitefly (aphids)

Bonsai are susceptible to the same insect pests as full-size trees. To help prevent infestation, the application of a systemic insecticide twice a year is beneficial. Systemic products are absorbed into the plant and give it protection for several months. A winter wash can be applied to deciduous trees to eliminate any overwintering eggs and grubs.

Vine weevil

The vine weevil grub can kill a tree quickly because it feeds on and destroys the roots. Treat with a soil insecticide at the first signs and if possible repot, making sure that all of the grubs are removed. The adult vine weevil hides away in rubbish, beneath pots and staging during the day, and emerges at night to eat large holes in the edges of leaves. Treat with an appropriate insecticide.

Vine weevil (Otiorhynchus sulcatus)

Vine weevil grub

Woolly aphid

Woolly aphid is a particular problem on beech and pine. It looks like a white, fluffy, sticky mass, and can be removed by spraying regularly with an insecticide.

Woolly aphid (Eriosoma lanigerum)

Red spider mite

Red spider mite is a tiny red insect which is not normally detected until very fine webs appear at the junctions of the trunk and branches. They often attack junipers, but can also cause a problem on many other trees, including indoor varieties. Treatment is in the form of an insecticide, which again can be applied on a regular basis.

Red spider mite (Acarina: Tetranychidae)

34

Diseases

Most diseases found in bonsai are the same as those which affect full-size trees and are mainly fungal infections, which can be reduced if hygienic practices are adhered to when preparing trees, pots and soil, and also with general cleanliness.

Routine spraying with systemic fungicides will control most of the common fungal infections. You may also spray with copper fungicide, alternating with the systemic variety, as an extra precaution.

Powdery mildew
Powdery mildew is a white dusty growth that appears on leaf surfaces and young stems, and can be treated by regular spraying with fungicide.

Powdery mildew

Damping off
Damping off is where seedlings begin to rot at the base of the stem, resulting in the seedling falling over and dying. Spray with copper-based fungicide.

Damping off

Rust
Rust appears on leaves as slightly raised orange/yellow spots and any affected leaves should be removed and destroyed. You should also spray with a zinc-based fungicide.

Rust

Verticillium wilt
Verticillium wilt is a disease that causes die-back in maples. It attacks the sapwood and is difficult to detect, and most trees should be treated with a systemic fungicide as a preventive measure.

Verticillium wilt

Peach leaf curl
Peach leaf curl can be a problem on trees of the Prunus family and appears as reddish-brown blistery shapes on the leaves. These quickly multiply, causing the leaves to curl up into distorted shapes. Treat with a copper-based fungicide.

Peach leaf curl

Grey mould
Grey mould is a fungus which occurs on leaves of plants that are kept in conditions of high humidity. It is possible to control by increasing ventilation and spraying with a systemic fungicide.

Grey mould

35

Formal Upright

The formal upright style of bonsai has a straight vertical trunk with the branches in fairly horizontal positions.

To create a formal upright shape, first assess which branches are best suited for the triangular design. Choose a thick branch as the lowest and then cut out any insignificant shoots, leaving a sufficient number to complete the design. If the trunk is not completely straight, apply a piece of wire of suitable thickness and manipulate the trunk until it is straight when viewed from the front. Viewed from the side, the trunk should be angled slightly to the rear as it rises from the soil, and slightly to the front in the upper part of the tree. Apply wire to the lowest branch, and after running the wire around the trunk one or more turns, wind it along the next branch up the trunk.

36

YOU WILL NEED
- rake
- soil
- pot
- scoop
- mesh
- branch cutters
- wire
- wire cutters
- scissors

BONSAI TIP
A good surface root system will give the base of the trunk a more mature look. Rake the soil away to expose the roots; this will enhance the appearance of the junction between the trunk and the soil.

1 Position the tree in the pot so that the trunk is vertical. Apply wire to the first, or lowest, branch you have chosen to retain.

2 Terminate the wire by bending it back on itself so that it secures the end of the branch. Cut off the excess wire, then continue with the next branch up the trunk.

3 Having wired all the branches, gently bend them all into horizontal positions.

4 Using scissors, trim all the shoot tips, so that the tree takes on a roughly triangular appearance when viewed from both the front and side.

Opposite: Juniperus chinensis

Informal Upright

Before any shaping work is carried out, the root base must be established. Inspect the roots by raking away the soil and study the shape of the tree from all sides. Having established the trunk angle, support the tree in this position.

YOU WILL NEED
- rake
- soil
- scoop
- pot
- mesh
- brick
- wire
- wire cutters
- scissors

38

This is one of the most common styles used in bonsai, probably because many full-size trees develop into this shape.

1 Check for the best trunk angle and prop up the pot with a brick.

2 Wire the trunk and bend into a gentle curve, then wire the branches and position them to give the tree a mature look.

3 Trim the long ends of the shoots with scissors. Note that the apex follows the same angle as that of the first, lower, part of the trunk.

Left: Cedrus deodara

Slanting

Establish the shape and health of the root system and decide which side is the front of the tree and whether the trunk would be better positioned at a different angle to look as natural as possible. The position of the branches must relate to the trunk, so that a mature shape is obtained. When a branch is to be placed in a drooping position, make sure that it bends down immediately at the junction with the trunk.

YOU WILL NEED
• rake
• soil
• scoop
• pot
• mesh
• branch cutters
• wire
• wire cutters

The slanting style is based on natural trees that have been affected by stormy weather and blown over at an angle.

1 Position the trunk at a slanting angle and remove the branch at the front.

2 Cut out the leading shoots with branch cutters and wire the branches.

39

3 Finish off the apex by bending it into a zigzag shape that complements the rest of the tree.

Right: Pinus thunbergii

Semi-cascade

Before shaping a bonsai tree into this style, first establish the shape and health of the root structure, which side should be the front and whether the angle of the trunk should be altered. Although the trunk line is initially upward, it very quickly bends over into a roughly horizontal position.

YOU WILL NEED
• rake
• soil
• scoop
• pot
• mesh
• branch cutters
• scissors
• wire
• wire cutters

40

The semi-cascade is a style that reflects the effect of difficult growing conditions on a tree. The styling here is designed to give the appearance of a tree growing out of the side of a rock face or quarry.

1 Position at the required angle by using extra soil in the bottom of the pot.

2 Trim the long shoots that hang down below the line of the trunk using branch cutters.

3 Remove the shoot that has grown back on itself with scissors.

4 Wire both the leading shoot and lower rear branch and bend them into place to create the basic shape.

5 Using scissors, remove any backward-growing branches. Finally, cut out the leading shoot.

Opposite: Cotoneaster

Cascade

As with all shaping methods, establish the shape and health of the roots, which side should be the front and whether the angle of the trunk should be altered.

YOU WILL NEED
- rake
- soil
- scoop
- pot
- mesh
- branch cutters
- scissors
- wire
- wire cutters

42

BONSAI TIP
A cascade should be grown in a deep pot, and displayed on a tall stand to complement its shape.

As with the semi-cascade style, the trunk line begins by growing vertically upward before cascading over the side of the pot. It represents a tree growing in a difficult situation, such as the side of a rock face.

1 Remove any branch that is growing in the opposite direction to the main cascade.

2 Trim any small branches from the lower trunk so that the cascading branch is seen to advantage.

3 Wire the trunk and trim out minor twigs, leaving only the main branches.

4 Continue wiring to the end of the trunk, then bend the trunk and trim off any remaining minor shoots.

Right: Juniperus procumbens

5 Wire the side branches and position so that a space, large enough to insert a hand, is left between them.

6 Prune the tail to length and trim excess shoots to give a mature look.

43

Windswept

Any conifer with a relatively straight trunk is suitable for styling into a windswept shape. Rake the soil away from the surface roots and check their appearance, to establish the best viewing angle. Lean the tree over to one side so that the best part of the trunk and roots are visible from the front, while at the same time taking the branch structure into account. Remove all or most of the branches on the windward side of the trunk. Decide which branches will give the most mature appearance, and remove the others. Position the remaining branches with wire so that a mature windswept appearance is achieved. The tree is then settled into the prepared pot, tied in, topped up with soil and watered.

44

YOU WILL NEED
- rake
- soil
- scoop
- pot
- mesh
- branch cutters
- scissors
- wire
- wire cutters

This style would be familiar to those who visit coastal or mountain areas, because it is based upon the form of full-size trees that have been constantly exposed to winds from one direction. These trees have branches only on the side of the trunk sheltered from the wind.

1 Using branch cutters, remove all branches that are growing in the opposite direction to the main trunk line to create a mature windswept appearance.

2 Position at the most appropriate angle and use scissors to remove all small twigs and branches.

3 Remove any upward-growing branches using branch cutters.

4 Trim off downward-growing branches to preserve the horizontal line of the style.

Above: Juniperus davurica

5 Wire the remaining branches.

6 Carefully bend branches so that they all flow in the same direction, as if they have been blown by constant winds.

BONSAI TIP

Do not carry out major work on both the top part of the tree and the roots at the same time. This could cause too much stress for the tree and may result in unwanted die-back in some areas.

Literati

The trunk is all-important for the literati shape. It is rarely straight and must have lots of "character". When selecting a tree, you may be able to buy something that has been damaged and is not really suitable for anything else. Rake the soil from the roots to establish their health and the best viewing angle. Make the branches droop severely to reflect the apparent age of the tree. A suitable pot would be circular and should not be too large.

YOU WILL NEED
- rake
- soil
- scoop
- pot
- mesh
- branch cutters
- wire
- wire cutters
- scissors

46

This style has a very tall, fairly thin trunk with just a few branches in the upper part of the tree. One can see the inspiration for this style in the wild where old pines have discarded their lower branches. Conifers tend to make the best literati bonsai.

1 Position the tree for the best trunk front; the line should be interesting and not totally straight.

2 Using branch cutters, remove some of the lower branches; characteristically, this style has most of its branches in the upper part of the tree.

3 Remove the heavier upper branches and most other small ones, leaving only about five main branches.

4 Wire the remaining branches. Position the branches to give a heavy, drooping appearance.

5 Use scissors to trim the branches so that a tidy, mature shape is achieved.

Opposite: Juniperus squamata

Twisted Trunk

The twisted trunk is not one of the most popular styles for bonsai because it does not represent a particularly natural appearance. The trunk takes the form of a spiral, which can be achieved by the use of thick wire to manipulate it into place. You will need a tree that has a fairly thick trunk which is flexible enough to be curved into the required form. Use a rake to scrape away the surface soil to check the health of the root system and to establish which is the best side to be the front. Select which branches will make a natural-looking tree.

YOU WILL NEED
- rake
- soil
- scoop
- pot
- mesh
- branch cutters
- scissors
- wire
- wire cutters

48

This style clearly has a strong Chinese connection, as many Chinese bonsai follow it. Ancient Chinese artefacts often bear paintings of trees like this.

1 Tilt the tree by resting the rear of the root ball on the back edge of the seed tray. This will give a better appearance to the line of the trunk.

2 Use branch cutters to remove branches covering the front of the tree and obscuring the trunk. Cut out all minor inner branches with a pair of scissors.

3 Using branch cutters, prune out any long uninteresting branches.

4 Wire the remaining branches and carefully bend into place. Trim away excessively long shoots to refine the outline.

Opposite: Pinus mugo

Broom

As full-size trees, this style can be seen in parks and gardens all over the world. Initially it was derived from the natural shape of several varieties of Zelkova trees. It is therefore best suited to these trees, but other species can be successfully grown in this style. The form is based around a straight section of trunk with the branches coming from the top. There may be a continuation of the initial part of the trunk, but it will taper fairly abruptly and have smaller branches emerging along its length.

YOU WILL NEED
• branch cutters
• scissors
• wire
• wire cutters

50

The broom style has an appearance similar to the traditional broom used for sweeping, made from a bunch of twigs tied to a wooden handle.

1 Turn the tree to find the best side to be the front; that is, the side with the most interesting trunk line.

2 Using branch cutters, remove the small, insignificant low branches.

3 Take out any branches that cross over another branch or the trunk.

4 Prune any heavy side branches.

5 Trim the excess length of the remaining side branches.

6 Wire any branches that need to be repositioned. Cut out the leading shoots on the apex.

Right: Acer palmatum

Forest or Group

To make a forest or group you can use a variety of trees, but you will find it easier to create a pleasing arrangement if you stick with the same species. In the wild, however, groups are often made up of mixed species, so give it a try – it can be very successful. It is important that the group is realistic and gives the impression of depth and perspective. When viewed from any direction, no three trees should be in a straight line and none of the trunks should be completely hidden behind another. Suitable pots would be shallow ovals or rectangles, but you can use a thin slab of slate or rock if you wish.

You will need
- rake
- soil
- scoop
- pot
- mesh
- branch cutters
- scissors

A forest or group is normally made up of at least five trees. The number should always be odd because this tends to give a more balanced appearance. Your arrangement must re-create the feeling of being in a forest, or copse.

1 Choose the dominant tree in the group and remove its lower branches with concave branch cutters. Having prepared the pot, position the main tree just right of centre.

2 Place the second-largest tree close to the main tree. You may have to trim some branches so that they sit close together, but not so close as to become confused with each other.

3 Complete the group with the remaining trees, keeping the smaller trees to the outside of the arrangement.

4 Trim back all remaining long shoots to give a tidy, balanced appearance.

Opposite: Larix leptolepis

Jin

In bonsai, the word *jin* refers to a dead branch that has lost its bark. If carried out correctly, the effect can be dramatic, creating a feeling of substantial age.

In the wild, dead branches would be exposed to rain and wind, and eventually be bleached silvery-white by the sun. This effect occurs naturally on many varieties of conifer, especially junipers and pines. Although dead branches do not appear on many deciduous trees, they can often be seen on oaks.

The best time to create *jin* is during the summer when the sap movement is at its greatest, because this makes the removal of the bark easier. When you have made the *jin*, leave it to dry in the sun before applying a coat of lime/sulphur, which will bleach and preserve the wood. This should be reapplied once or twice a year during the summer to maintain the weather resistance of the *jin*. The *jin* can then be refined by carving and smoothing with fine sandpaper until a truly natural effect is achieved. Remember that the *jin* must always be in proportion to the other branches with foliage.

YOU WILL NEED
• branch cutters
• knife
• pliers

54

1 Using branch cutters, cut off the branches to be *jinned*, leaving long stumps.

2 Cut around the bark at the base of each stump using a knife, and slit the bark to the end of each stump.

3 Lift the bark with the tip of the knife and peel it off.

4 The ends can now be broken back with pliers to give a natural, weathered look to the stumps.

Opposite: Larix leptolepis

Suitable Varieties

Whether bonsai trees become known as indoor or outdoor plants, depends on the area of the world in which they are going to be grown.

This book generally deals with trees that are hardy when kept outdoors in a temperate climate. Bonsai should not be subjected to deep freezing – below -4ºC (25ºF) – which is why in cold winter regions they need the protection of a greenhouse or cold frame. When trees are referred to as indoor trees in this book, it means that they must be kept in a more controlled environment, such as in a house or greenhouse. They will usually need additional warmth and humidity to maintain a healthy growth pattern. They may also be kept outside during the summer when, and if, the climate comes close to the original climatic conditions in which the plant grows naturally.

In some ways it would be true to say that there is no such thing as indoor bonsai, because the type of material that is used has its origins as a plant that grows outside in the natural environment.

HOW TO OBTAIN INDOOR BONSAI
Suitable material for indoor bonsai can be bought at almost any garden centre or supermarket. Tropical or sub-tropical plants that are used as house-plants can often be turned into bonsai. These plants are normally those that have a wealth of green leaves as their dominant feature, but you should always check the trunk to consider whether it would look good when transformed into a tree-like form. You will have to use your imagination to decide if your choice will be suitable as a bonsai.

WHICH SPECIES TO USE
Species used for indoor bonsai vary considerably, and some of the most popular are the many varieties of Ficus or fig, the most common of these being *Ficus benjamina* and *Ficus retusa*. Other species used are *Crassula arborescens*, *Nandina domestica*, *Serissa foetida*, *Punica granatum*, as well as *Sageretia theezans*, *Aralia elegantissima*, *Myrtus communis*, fuchsias, gardenias and many more.

INDOOR BONSAI CARE
Trees grown indoors may need more frequent checking of the climatic conditions. Good light is essential for indoor bonsai. This can be provided by using grow lights to supplement the

available natural light. Make sure the soil is always kept moist. Spray the foliage regularly to maintain a fairly high humidity to help keep the leaves in a good healthy condition.

Opposite: Sageretia theezans *after trimming and shaping.*

Above: Sageretia theezans *is a popular species for indoor bonsai and specimens are normally sold as fully trained trees. This one has grown on and lost its original shape: the long shoots need to be cut back, leaving just one or two leaves.*

Left: Commonly known as the money tree or jade plant, Crassula arborescens *is often underestimated as bonsai material. When controlling its growth, wait until two or three pairs of leaves have been produced and then trim back to one pair. Each pruned shoot will produce two new shoots.*

Ficus wiandii

Regular misting of the foliage with water is beneficial and the soil should be kept just moist at all times. Feed lightly, but regularly, during the main growing season from spring to autumn. As shoots grow, prune them back to one or two leaves.

YOU WILL NEED
- rake
- soil
- scoop
- pot
- mesh
- branch cutters
- wound sealer
- wire
- wire cutters

58

The *Ficus wiandii* has a compact growth habit with well-proportioned leaves. Plants may have one or more trunks and generally have an interesting root system.

1 Choose the most interesting trunk line. The best position for this tree is with the largest trunk towards the front. Using branch cutters, remove the crossover branch.

2 Cut off any inner branches that do not follow the line. Any white fluid from the wounds will dry up and the wounds should be covered with wound sealer.

3 Remove any heavy upward-growing branches from the tree.

4 Wire the remaining branches.

5 Bend the branches into place, making sure that the branch angles are complementary.

Opposite: Ficus wiandii

Aralia elegantissima

When grown in a group, always make sure that the tallest plant is somewhere in the central third of the arrangement, and that the rest of the plants get progressively smaller towards the sides and rear.

YOU WILL NEED
- rake
- soil
- scoop
- pot
- mesh
- scissors
- rocks or tufa

60

These plants, commonly known as finger aralia, can have one or more trunks and make a very attractive landscape.

1 Cut off the lower and inner leaves of the plants using scissors.

2 Place in the prepared pot, arranging the seven trunks so that they are slightly spread out at the top.

BONSAI TIP
It is important to mist regularly as the leaves can dry out quickly.

3 Add extra soil until the trees are firmly potted.

4 Carefully position several pieces of rock or tufa to give the effect of a miniature landscape.

Opposite: Aralia elegantissima

Myrtus communis

Don't be tempted to "clip" the foliage; that would be topiary rather than bonsai. Thin out the top growth to achieve a branched structure – be persistent as the dense foliage mass can quickly regrow. This species requires regular misting with water to maintain the health of the foliage, particularly in the summer months. Water when the soil begins to show signs of drying, and never allow the roots to stand in water as they will quickly rot. Good light is important, but avoid direct sunlight.

YOU WILL NEED
• rake
• soil
• scoop
• pot
• mesh
• scissors
• rocks or tufa

62

Commonly known as dwarf myrtle, only young plants of this variety are usually available, but they are easy to train.

1 Having removed the plants from their pots, rake away the soil to obtain a suitable root ball and expose the trunk base. Using scissors, trim off some of the lower branches so that the trunk lines can be seen.

2 Trim each plant into a tree-like form.

3 Prepare the pot in the normal way and add a layer of soil. Arrange some rocks, in this case tufa, so that there is enough space to plant trees around them and add extra soil.

4 Place the medium-size tree on the left and settle it into the soil. Place the smallest tree on the right.

5 Plant the largest beside it and to the right of the rock. Make sure that this tree is slightly higher than the others.

Opposite: Myrtus communis

Index